Cirrus Clouds

Poems of Travelling and Social Justice

Gill Hague
2015

Published by Tangent Books
in association with Rive Gauche Publishing

Tangent Books

RIVE GAUCHE PUBLISHING

Cirrus Clouds Poems of Travelling and Social Justice
by Gill Hague

First published 2015 by Tangent Books
in association with Rive Gauche Publishing

Tangent Books
Unit 5.16 Paintworks, Bristol, BS4 3EH
0117 972 0645
www.tangentbooks.co.uk
Email: richard@tangentbooks.co.uk

ISBN 978-1-910089-18-7

Design: Joe Burt (joe@wildsparkdesign.co.uk)

Cover photographs: Cirrus clouds above rural Québec,
by Cherry van Son (taken near Scotstown in the Eastern
Townships, Québec, Canada)

These poems are dedicated

to my late mother

to my dear friends

and to poets and activists
for social justice and liberation everywhere

With thanks

With deep thanks: to Rachel Bentham, Rive Gauche, for help, editing and support. To the late Pat VT West, original founder of Rive Gauche. To my various supportive publishing, editing and formatting advisers, particularly Richard Jones of Tangent Books and Joe Burt, designer. To dear, dear friends across the world, most especially my treasured compañeras, Alison Assiter and Cherry van Son. Thanks also to Cherry for the cover photographs, used as a tribute to her endless creativity.

My thanks to the Centre for Gender and Violence Research, University of Bristol, which Ellen Malos and I founded in 1990. To all the wonderful activists / researchers with whom I have worked internationally and nationally for comments, support and permissions. Especially to my dear colleagues, Ravi Thiara and Nazand Begikhani. And with sincerest thanks for helpful input to Geetanjali Gangoli, Lynn Sardinha, Gene Feder, Shahana Rasool, Nishi Mitra, Kathy Willis, Ann Harvey and at Mifumi: Atuki Turner, Patrick Ndira, Evelyn Schiller, Immaculate and Jane-Rose.

My love and gratitude to Justice Albie Sachs, previously Constitutional Judge in the Constitutional Court of South Africa. To Corinne Oosthuizen of Agape. To my friends, Renée Despres, Lynne Miller, Larry Simon, Frances Madeson, Margaret Cerullo, Shirley Brown and Mary Woods for helpful input. And for general support, to Jac Gruhn, Harriet Wordsworth and Leticia Mujeni. For both love and useful comments always, to Cassie Hague, Keiran Merrick, René-François Bordes, and, most of all, Dave Merrick. Special hugs to recently-arrived Ezra Bordes.

With great love to the late Dorothy and Tom Williamson.

Contents

Preface by Rachel Bentham,
Rive Gauche

Gill Hague has made it her life's work to combat violence against women, but these poems include issues relating to social justice more generally. Along with Ellen Malos and many dedicated others, Gill has had an internationally important role in both political activism on domestic violence and partner abuse, and in creating a body of research and publications documenting these issues, which serves to underpin ongoing campaigns for social equality. Tirelessly, she has travelled the globe to publicise, support and further this crucial cause.

Reading this varied collection, it is clear she has found it both humbling and inspiring to meet with so many people struggling and working to end social inequality and abuse of women. These poems honour women, men, and young people, and the places and practices they have created in different parts of the globe, often in the context of extreme personal danger and threats to themselves and their families. Their daily heroism is acknowledged, celebrated and honoured.

Gill has been writing poetry for over forty years, often commemorating events in her personal life, and here, characteristically, she pays tribute to others. These poems contain many lovely phrases like 'glittering with youth' (*Graduation at the University of Sulaimaniya p. 13*), but more than that, they reveal both self-awareness and an acute consciousness of her 'western' gaze. Through her sensitivity to other cultural conventions she points to some sweet ironies: 'contrary to the customs of/public behaviour/that were carefully explained to me/[they] are busy/looking into each other's eyes/and holding hands' (*South Bombay p.33*).

There is a sense of many different places in this collection, seen within the context of their particular political and social challenges, yet presented as poignant vignettes, as in 'the fragile, precious flower of protest' (*The poets and demonstrations p.24*), in which Kurdish poets gather, smoke, eat and talk. Often there is a telling juxtaposition of politics with other features of ordinary life, for instance, her depiction of children playing in the poem entitled '*They don't know yet' (p.26*).

Yet this is far from an assembly of laments. Above all, again and again, Gill points to the positive, describing places like *Agape* in South Africa, revealing her respect and honour for the people quietly and stoically developing ways to cope with and work through deep emotional pain, and also founding new and inclusive communities. In all the places and poems of course there is struggle and suffering, and also there is inspiration and admiration. 'You are doing it/without being able to read/any of the famous books' (*For the Women p.92*). Above all, there is love for others, always others. As Gill states, the subjects of her poems are 'heroes and beacons to all around you' (*To Jane-Rose and Immaculate, the respected elders of the activists p.96*).

Cirrus Clouds and Social Justice: Introduction

And they, the days, made us.
And thus we were born,
The children of the days,
The discoverers,
Life's searchers.

Eduardo Galeano[1]

Eduardo Galeano was and will remain world-renowned as a Latin American writer, historian, cultural activist and ground-breaker, often characterised as being a moral and political compass for our time. He was quoting here from an ancient Mayan interpretation of humanity, in his 2013 book, *Children of the Days: A Calendar of Human History*. It is to our huge loss that he sadly died in April 2015. I was privileged to learn from him during the preparation of this book.

*****

Cirrus clouds and journeys gave rise to the idea of this collection of poetry from different countries, with a human justice focus. Eduardo Galeano's contemporary, Derek Walcott, the Caribbean poet and winner of the 1992 Nobel Prize for Literature, has spoken often of cirrus clouds, those hair-thin wisps of cloud we sometimes see very high in the sky. He talks of them, in his extraordinary poetry, as carriers of ideas, of feelings, of understandings of the world, drifting from one place to another. Walcott's book-length poem, *Omeros*,[2]

1   Galeano, Eduardo (2013) *Children of the Days: A Calendar of Human History*, New York: Nation Books.

2   Walcott, Derek (1990) *Omeros*, London: Faber and Faber.

for example, wafts the stories of Homer's Iliad to a post-colonial, impoverished village in the Caribbean island of St. Lucia -- like cirrus clouds, he tells us.

While the poems here cannot be compared with the exhilarating works of Galeano and Walcott, they have grown out of this metaphor of cirrus clouds. They transport experiences from countries around the world, ranging from India to Greece, from the Kurdistan Region of Iraq to Malaysia to the US to Uganda, starting out from my home in Bristol, UK. Some of the more lengthy poems are written as tributes to extraordinary individuals and projects, including *Agape*, a unique South African township mental health project, and *Mifumi* in Uganda, leading Africa and, in some ways, the world in combating violence against women.

The poems reflect on and celebrate these various countries, people and interactions through a lens informed by commitment to social justice, to women's and human rights, and to liberation.

This is not conventional or classic 'grand' poetry. Rather, it is in the specific sub-genre of travel writing or travel poems. Some of it is 'reportage', providing information about the country concerned, occasionally lightly and with a degree of irony, or in the form of longer prose pieces. The journeys concerned were taken over many years, and the poems record real situations and events that actually happened.

In 2012, I retired from the Centre for Gender and Violence Research, University of Bristol. I was one of the two founder members, 25 years ago, of this Centre. My role has been as an activist, author, researcher and Professor (of Violence Against Women Studies), working, nationally and internationally, to challenge the human tragedy of the abuses and violations that women experience across the globe.

Thus there is inevitably some attention in the collection to violence against women issues. It needs to be stressed at the outset, though, that exposing these issues in a named country does not mean they can be regarded as in any way specific to that country or region. All the types of gender violence raised in the poems occur widely across the world. The same is true for issues of poverty and discrimination.

Overall then, the collection is travel poetry, but with a dedication to social change and to trying to combat inhumanity and injustice.

The wonderfulness of the world despite its injustices, and the enrichment and education to be gained from experiencing journeys, countries and people, is what underlies this book. Using the image of wisps of cirrus clouds as they drift high above us, I hope you may enjoy sharing these journeys, celebrating places -- but also human beings in their extraordinary valour.

Gill Hague, 2015

*****

The Sections of the Book

We read, we travel, we become.

Derek Walcott[3]

I have used these things to say what is, to me, the wideness and the wonder of the world.

Georgia O'Keeffe[4]

The first section of the collection starts by reflecting, as a sort of taster, on a few very different places, all revisited later in the book. The initial poem honours the pavement people of Indian cities, followed by poems from Greece, Iraqi Kurdistan and Uganda.

In subsequent sections, a few words of explanation or introduction are included where needed to contextualise the poems. There are also a few footnotes, uncommon in poetry collections but used here to provide additional background and information about the country concerned.

The poems are grouped by place, including Cuba, South Africa, Malta, the US, Malaysia, Canada, Spain, Mexico, the UK, and, in India: Kerala, Bombay and Rajasthan. The final short section contains poems of resolution.

---

3   Walcott, Derek (2004) *The Prodigal,* New York: Farrar, Straus.
4   O'Keeffe, Georgia, words from 1976, Georgia O'Keeffe Museum, Santa Fe, New Mexico.

Section I
Poems to start

Last month, they were driven out with batons

I walk late in this city.
The people who live on the pavements
say goodnight to me,
cooking chapatis
or arranging cardboard bedding,
children asleep, just in vests.

Some families sit watching
a blurred TV
plugged in somehow
to the city's electricity.
Last month, they were driven out
with batons.

Now, a security guard
with a big rifle
grins and watches with them.
It's cricket, that's why,
the Test between India
and Pakistan.

******

I always stop to speak with
a small, deformed man near the junction.
We know each other a little
across the huge barriers.

His height is about three feet
but he doesn't stand.

Whenever he sees me,
he shouts and shouts,
bursting into smiles,
and waves me over,
lying on the ground, propped up.
I squat beside him.

We talk together between our languages.
It's the third year now,
we've met each day I'm here.
He says he is happy,
living and sleeping,
every day and every night,

on this three-yard stretch of concrete.
There might be some
protection going on.
Any number of others, he says,
would want to snatch the space.
He's cleaned up the rubbish,

beds down with laughter,
amid the noise and traffic fumes.
It's his own neat corner
of the grimy pavement.

The fourth year, I rush, smiling,
dodging through the crowds,
looking forward
to seeing him, excited

but he's gone without trace.

Graduation at the University of Sulaimaniya in Iraqi Kurdistan[5]

This poem was written before the rise of the Jihadists in 2014. While the future of this Region may be threatened and the danger is considerable at the time of writing, life goes on as usual for most people, and Iraqi Kurdistan seems to be -- at least for now – moderately secure.

These people, so young with eager faces,
new graduates all, starting out on life.

They wear traditional Kurdish clothes today.
The boys have gelled
their shiny black hair solid.
The girls wear extra-high heels
and sparkle in customary full-length garments,
with gold and sequins.

Many of them have sculpted their hair
with layers of curls,
a pretty scarf balanced on top
as a nod, for some, to being Muslim.

They have big collective photographs taken
with their esteemed teachers.
Each photo takes at least half an hour.
There are flowers, much laughter.
I hold back the tears.

5   For further contextualising information about Iraqi Kurdistan Region, see the short section of poems on Kurdistan in Section II, from page 22.

II

Excitement fills the air,
these gleaming young people
graduating from their
fine Kurdish university,
that takes 50% women as a policy,
with its
free teaching,
free books,
free housing,
free food,
no fees.
They are fairly certain to get jobs apparently,
most are hoping to marry and be happy.

They are the new Kurdistan,
Iraqi Kurdistan.

As they glow today on their sea of pride,
it can be hard to recall
that just a few years ago
they might have been freedom fighters,

or to remember, perhaps,
about the genocides,
the concentration camps,
the expulsions,
the incarcerations,
the gassing,
the burned villages,
the deaths,
the wars....
For them, it's normal, some tell me,
to have such a past.

They are not dwelling on it.
They laugh
and rush about,
glittering with youth.

III

Let them be happy then.
Let those traumas
that scar their great country
rest

on this joyous day.
They are the new Kurdistan.
I hold back the tears.

Go with delight, dear students.

But perhaps the family members
killed,
tortured,
imprisoned,
gassed,
lost in genocidal attacks
or imposed wars,
that they almost certainly have,
live on quietly,
deep in their young and optimistic hearts.

The pink lilo

Set in the Pagasitic Gulf of the Aegean Sea, Greece.

We blew up the lilo,
pink and transparent.
It looked rather disgusting.
It floated well though,
suddenly getting away from us
and dancing across the bay
before the slight warm breeze.

We swam like crazy to catch it,
anticipating a full-scale
tourist drowning alert.

The lilo bobbed on and on,
mocking and swollen.
Through binoculars,
we saw it land

way out on the abandoned island,
harsh and dry, the only place
the ancient monks

had dared to live, protected
from persecutors by the sea,
their lives contained,
pared to the bone.

*****

Later, in the twilight,

ghost monks crept down to the beach.
They were intrigued.

Fumbling with excitement,
they carried
the unpleasantly translucent pink throne
into their ruined buildings,

encrusted grey among the olives.
Then they took turns to sit on it
grandly.

Our hotel, it's seen better days

This light poem was written in a decaying hotel in Eastern Uganda, near the Kenyan border, while working there with a South Asian UK colleague and our Ugandan partners (see the later poems from Uganda).

A faintly scabby steam-room,
we sometimes come to here,
a luxury though,
full of African men with power
and prosperous stomachs
that stick out.
Most of them work for the UN.
(There's a temporary Refugee Camp
up the road.[6])

The gardens are delightful
in both sun and moon,
with flamboyant trees, lilies, jacaranda.
After dark, a large bat, like an owl,
nearly collides with me,
but thank goodness
for that super-radar business.
I jump theatrically anyway.

Inside, rail-thin waiters who live in the hotel,
young men,
far from home and lonely,
are talked down to
by born-again white Christians
from Alabama

6   This was at a time of temporary unrest in neighbouring areas across the border in Kenya.

come to convert
the already very Christian locals.

Of course I'd prefer if I was
the only white person around.
So I could show
that whites can come here
and not try to impose things,
that solidarity and a different humanity are possible

as I try to stretch across the
ragged gulfs
of the colonialist past
to join hearts and hands.

So how pretentious is *that*...

II

Just getting through the long days
takes some doing,
as we get a bit dizzy and overheated,
always encased in deadly bug killer.

There's *African Idol* on the television
or Arsenal v. Manchester United.
The power goes off and on.
You get used to it.
What makes anyone think
non-stop electricity a right?

At the gate, the watchman strolls slowly round
with a massive gun --
although one from a previous generation.
He wears a battered uniform and is frightening.

Then he starts chatting.
He tells me he works 16 hours every single day.

Once a month, he says, he has one day off,
cycles 25 miles to see his wife and children
for three or four hours,
and cycles 25 miles back.

III

He grins, nodding up for us
at the golden weaverbirds.
They are clever at lining their nests with
bright green grass, making a big racket.

We, though, keep a very strict lookout for snakes.
Night-time flying insects and giant millipedes
we are not at all keen on either.
Coming from the UK, we are more scared of them
than the gun of course
(a silliness which would never be the case
for the "sensibly scared-of-loaded-firearms" local people).

And that sweet African air
can get filled with diesel fumes
as ancient trucks lumber by
in clouds of smoke and dust
bringing Uganda's oil from Mombasa.

But still it is
that sweet African air, shimmering
around the now-privatised cement-works
that used to support all the town,
fading to the fine far mountains.

Section II
Poems grouped by country

Pelion, where the Centaurs wandered

Greece has been forced to go broke and bravely fight back,
but it's a country and a half, isn't it.
Down in Pelion, where the Centaurs wandered,
the women visitors used to all jump into
the soft water, laughing to each other.

They would drink honey-wine all afternoon,
eat fat Greek tomatoes with bread
and feta, which the grocer kept in a slab
in a wooden drawer and would cut for them,
leaning over it with the long ash of his cigarette
drooping from his lips.

They talked of how humans can nurture each other,
discussed the fine social movements
they had given their lives to,
movements of women
transforming the world everywhere.

They heard owls
and they mixed yogurt with honey and walnuts.
The women spent whole days in the white sun,
swimming and sunbathing,
getting slightly drunk,
reflecting with a sense of warmth on their shared pasts.

The Centaurs had no time for women naturally.
Lucky then that they had disappeared.

Iraqi Kurdistan

The various poems about the autonomous Kurdistan Region[7] in northern Iraq in this collection were written during visits with colleagues, led by well-known Kurdish gender expert, feminist activist and internationally renowned poet, Nazand Begikhani. The projects include collaboratively developing an Action Plan on 'Honour'-based Violence and Killing, and also establishing issues related to gender as worthy to be considered, researched and studied within various universities. These have all been 'first time ever' initiatives in the Region.

Note: The great Kurdish poet, Sherko Bekas, recognised as the most famous in Kurdistan, features anonymously in the following poem. He tragically died in 2013, during the preparation of this collection. After discussion with key poets and others in Kurdistan, the decision was made to include his name and to continue to present this poem (with its slightly humorous observations about smoking, of which he would have approved). The poem is included with respect and thanks for the thrilling, transformatory and progressive poetry he left us, and his contribution and dedication to building a new Iraqi Kurdistan.

---

7   The semi-independent, autonomous region of Iraqi Kurdistan lies in the North of Iraq and has a different history, both recent and ancient, from Iraq 'proper'. It is part of the wider area of Kurdistan (the 'land of Kurds') which is not currently recognised as an independent State, but crosses the State borders of all the surrounding countries: Turkey, Syria, Iran, Iraq and the formerly Soviet republics of Armenia and Azerbaijan. A stable area with civil society flourishing, it presently faces Jihadist threat (see also p. 11) and has taken in huge numbers of refugees, increasing the population of 4 - 5 million by about a third (at least 1.5 million people) at the time of writing.

The poets and demonstrations
(cirrus clouds from the Arab uprisings)

Although, it should be noted, these campaigners and poets are proudly
Kurdish and resent the forced Arabisation they previously endured.

The poets are welcoming back
an old and dear friend
from exile in Europe.
Human warmth and
Kurdish-style eye-contact fill the spaces.
It feels generous.
We sit eating mezze and
drinking wine somewhat subversively.
There are babies crying
and families all around.

Mainly we talk of the demonstrations.
The poets have been there.
They make sure they are part of these things.

They are at the edge
where poets should always be, by definition.

II

These unexpected student demonstrations
for more freedom, democracy,
follow the other Middle Eastern uprisings
(but here in a place
already trying, at least a bit.)

They've now been going on for exuberant months.

The police attacked today in clashes,
agents provocateurs perhaps.
You can never tell quite what is going on.
We'd heard gunfire,
the student camp torn down.
A boy shot dead.
He was twelve.

They are sad and disappointed
these Kurdish poets who love their homeland.

The fragile, precious flower
of people's protest
seems to be getting swallowed up.

III

The most famous poet of all
speaks with authority.
Everyone always listens.
He is well-known everywhere.
Strangers keep arriving at his side
to greet him.

He chain smokes.
It's hard for him to fit in that mezze.
(He manages by taking quick bites between
gasping in the streams of smoke.)

Everyone is worried about fundamentalist Islamism
in this unsure almost-country,
still trying to heal from the wars,
the bombs filled with lethal chemicals.

A delicate juddering type of healing it is,

the factions still in conflict sometimes.

The poets look gloomy
and sit smoking.

IV

There are secrets in the room too.
There have to be.

But then there are gales of laughter,
shrugs about ageing love affairs,
sudden explosions of photo-taking
and lamb shish arriving,
talk of art and humanity at its best.
The most famous poet,
in a place that honours its poets,
pays for everyone else.
It's no good trying to argue about it.

Never far away
are those jarring dislocations
across continents.

More wine clearly.
The poets enjoy the wine.

There are harsh severings to come, yet again.
These fine people are used to that.
They've had to be
in their long and scarred journey.

Some issues referred to in the following poem are distressing but it is important to emphasise again that violence against women, including in the name of 'honour', and other forms of gender discrimination, occur widely across the countries of the world and are in no way confined to the Middle East or other specific regions, or to any particular religion or culture.

They don't know yet

We eat at the table with fresh herbs
and piles of vegetables, soft with fragrance,
talking about the dramatic scope
of Kurdish and Near East politics.
Two children play around us.

They belong to a big extended family
at the table next door.
Their mothers gesticulate at them
from time to time.

A boy and a girl.
She dominates the play in a sweet way.
He giggles, following her with adulation in his eyes,
laughing and tumbling together.

They don't know yet
that in the future
she will probably have to obey him,
her younger male relative,
be a virgin at marriage,
always dress with decorum,
tend to the needs of men as her first priority,
never go out of the house in the evening
unless with male kin.
He will probably have free range.

She lives in the city so
things have got much better,
but in many places
she could still be punished
in the name of honour.
We met the relatives of several victims
killed through burning,
talked with a woman whose nose
had been cut off.

Not anymore though.

Things are on the move
with the dedication and vigilance
of courageous women activists
who stand up to religious and
conservative condemnation,
who keep on going,
despite fatwas against them,
despite hostile media that shames them by name,
despite death threats,
in this traumatised country, sprouting anew.

They are making changes,
building a new consensus,
winning the battle.

A boy and a girl.
For now,
she dominates the play in a sweet way.
He giggles, following her with adulation in his eyes,
laughing and tumbling together.

The poems from different parts of India throughout this collection were written during visits to work jointly with Indian and British South Asian colleagues, conducting activist and research projects on gendered violence e.g. in 'slum' communities, in schools, in relation to immigration to the UK, and in terms of developing previously untried collaborative transnational teaching. The first section on Bombay is followed by later sections set in Kerala and Rajasthan.

Back to Bombay

The old name with a whiff of colonialism and tradition, but still so-called by progressives, human rights advocates and feminists. Now Mumbai, renamed by rightwing cultural nationalists.

Outside these places of social work learning: an India / UK exchange

Outside their place of social work learning,
you can buy coconuts to drink
and pani puri.
Outside our one, on the other hand,
there are daffodils and early Victorian houses

built in the days of the slave trade.
In front of theirs,
the frangipani is flowering,
ancient sewing machines
rattle on the roadside.

Cobblers will mend your shoes and umbrellas
(that any UK shop would
thoughtlessly chuck out),
the soles of their feet pressed together

to provide both last and vice.

They'll charge about 40 rupees.
In our place, on the other hand,
it costs 300 rupees for a cup of coffee.
It is too cold here.
We have to keep rubbing our visitors' hands.

They think of social work as progressive change,
as emancipation and empowerment.
Their social work projects are social action ones.
Ours more usually are bureaucratic social control.
Nevertheless we galvanise each other.

We have more in common than not
as we devise ways to deal with
men's violence,
as we dream of
a world where women and children are safe.

Western eyes

The man barks after me,
aggressively,
like men too often do.

I speed up to get away
not meeting his eye
like women always have.

His shouts follow me
and I start to sweat.
I can hear my heart pounding.

This has happened before.

I hope I can outpace him
and, when I turn around,
he won't be there anymore.

I'll have got away.

Men controlling the streets,
you could say.
Yes, you could say that.

*****

This man shuffles on one side
and stretches out his hands to me
like big hardened shovels.

Where fingers should be,
he has black lumps,

cracked and rotting.

The leprosy would be controlled these days.

This wouldn't happen now.
It wouldn't happen to his friend either
who has disturbingly angled limbs.

He gets about fast on a trolley.

Apparently, he was professionally modified
by his beggar master many years ago.
The beggar master paid

good money to have it done.
But it has been a lucrative modification.
I feel ill, of course,

in a stupid, privileged way.
I make a point
of giving them something,

and then feel noble and good.
That is if I can't get away
with pretending I haven't seen them.

It cost me 70,000 rupees
to come here to my great enrichment.
Anyway, I give them

5 rupees each.

South Bombay

Sophisticated Bombay
young women,
not a sari between them,
are sipping gaspacho
and fresh juices
outside the voguish coffee house.

They are being rather rude
to the pavement dwellers
and street children who slide
among them, ever hopeful.
I walk a bit nervously
towards Back Bay.

Its lace of lights still gets called
the 'Queen's Necklace',
Victoria of course,
those imperialists again.
It stops your heart
with its glowingness.

The clasp of the necklace
is at Malabar Hill, looking over the bay
where the great mansions
the British built
need a coat or two
of paint these day.

That fabled Arabian Sea is grey,
a false mistress really.
It smells a bit,
impossible for it not to.

Poor great city –
it's a tall order, after all,

to expect it to squeeze its millions
into a long thin peninsula,
half of it reclaimed from the sea.
What kind of shape for a city is that?
A scorpion's tail,
as Rushdie has it.

But Back Bay attracts everyone
in the evening when it's cooler.
There is street food
at Chowpatty where someone
might give you a cheap head massage
on the dark beach.

There are jasmine flowers in garlands,
tired men on bikes
serving chai
out of panniers,
and grinning couples
sitting on the long sea-wall,

who, contrary to the customs of
public behaviour
that were carefully explained to me,
are busy
looking into each other's eyes
and holding hands.

Another poem from Greece

Greece and democracy

Is it the lapping of the Aegean,
these breezes like the lyre,
these silver-grey olive groves
that once made a few people
have the first-ever
idea of a new society?
They gave it the name 'democracy'.[8]

Could it have happened
in harsher climes
where the weather would kill you
as soon as look at you.

In equatorial extremes, for instance,
where day becomes night in seconds
and brutal fevers lurk.

Could it have happened in rasping deserts
that choke you with dust.

In icy wastelands
where it is dark for half the year.

---

8   We know that different groups of people across the world had often previously lived
using collective structures or setting up proto-democracies. But Greece was probably the
first place to systematise this way of decision-making.

It could have.
But it didn't.

No, it was here,
in the land of tamarisk,
olives and lemons,
turquoise seas,
and the making of honey (even back then).

Here, in this warm place
that the first glimmer of
the idea of the people --
the 'demos' --
having the power --
the 'kratos' --
to rule or govern,
stumbled into flawed
human plans.

Those Grecian glimmers
of democracy
weren't that great of course,
the majority excluded,
slaves,
the impoverished,
all women.

but look what they started off.

We'll get there yet just maybe.

Uganda

This poem was produced as a public tribute to the NGO, Mifumi, and then given to the organisation and used to support its work.

My UK colleague, Ravi Thiara, and I have collaborated with Mifumi for some years on participatory action and other projects. Mifumi works to combat both violence against women and poverty in Uganda and across Africa, with centres in various Ugandan locations and in the UK. The organisation is world-leading in developing understandings of, and work on, bride-price (payment by men for wives at marriage) and its frequent connection to the violation of women.

With thanks to Mifumi Executive Director, Atuki Turner, Senior Directors, Evelyn Schiller and Patrick Ndira, and other key staff, past and present, particularly Mary Gorretti Ajoot and Janet Otte, who showed us endless generosity. The name of the NGO is placed in capitals in this poem, as advocated by the organisation. This tribute, laid out for publicity purposes by staff members, and the later related poems, are used here with the agreement of Mifumi.

Thank you, MIFUMI: a public tribute

Well,
you are an inspiration to us all,
MIFUMI.
Everyone says so.
It almost becomes glib,
but actually it's true.

Here,
village women who have experienced
gut-churning violence from men
have changed,
have become organisers,

sing and dance,
take care
of other survivors,
holding each other up,
strong together,
always together.

There are domestic abuse advice centres,
advocates to combat sexual violence,
women's micro-loan schemes,
sewing courses and counselling,
community forums
and
and a strengthening of the people.

You even built a needed police station,
repaired a broken bridge to the village.

I join all those others
in being so proud,

fiercely proud,

to be linked
a little bit with you,
with all you have achieved,
through your activism
and dignity
and compassion
and resolution.

I can see how the odds
are stacked against you,

as you fight doggedly on the side of

violated women,

as you lead the world on bride price
and its links with domestic violence --
but can be vilified
and physically attacked
in some local places here
of cultural conflict.

II

Yet,
you are transforming things
despite those critics
who have not the imagination
to see what a human gift
they have on their doorstep.

At your simple Health Centre,
women with babies on their laps
wait in crouched groups for hours,
having walked for hours and hours more,
to see the doctor.
But all of those babies
are having immunisations.
People are learning
what causes malaria.
Minor operations are possible.
There is HIV testing.

And what was here before?
Where did they all go then?

You have brought
something extraordinary,

growing out of a deep past tragedy

that still floats through your work
from time to time
like a wisp of cirrus cloud.

III

In your domestic violence centres,
what you do is
give the women
new strength and possibilities.

Lots of the men don't like it of course.

They know they lose some of their dominance
when the women start challenging it.
And that is exactly what is happening.

The women stay brave though,
despite severe threats and danger,
taking survivors in to sleep on their mud floors,
setting up groups in villages,
singing the songs.

IV

And you do it for the children too.
They are bright-eyed,
so keen to learn.
They glow and shine
in this unexpected school of theirs,
made by you, MIFUMI,

where previously there was nothing.

Your
pioneering school and health centre,
pioneering domestic violence services,
pioneering bride price work.

Your constitutional and policy challenges
with governments.
Your unique African women's refuges.

Your unprecedented radio programmes,
this first-ever men's project.

Hard and glorious acts of bravery,
hard and glorious acts of challenge

in a warm family of international
supporters and activists
conjuring great human leaps
of social change.

Tread with care and with strength,
wondrous MIFUMI.

Africa
and the world
cannot thrive without you.

Poems and prose in the US

The selection of US poems and prose stems from visits for gender violence work and to see old and new friends (especially on the East Coast). The New Mexican poems were written during extended periods living in the State, mainly close to the small State capital, Santa Fe, the oldest capital in the United States (established when Spanish colonisation of the land that became the South West expanded northwards from colonised Mexico).

Homage to New York City

New York, New York, it's a wonderful town.
Well, it was then and it is now.
Everyone visiting gets excited
when they first see it,
the city of cities.
Thirty years ago, a New Yorker friend said
more things happen to you
in 10 minutes in NYC
than in a week anywhere else.
Well, it was true then and it is now.

*****

Some of the greatest left-wing intellectuals
of our age are here,
the greatest buildings clearly,
the greatest in-line skating in Central Park,
wild skateboarding,
the Lesbian and Gay Pride marches,
Latino carnivals,
Charlie Parker festivals,
graffiti gardens and poets on E 4th St.

II

Homage:
In Washington Square Park,
you can watch champion-level
chess players
on the very edge of destitution
playing open-air chess games
at express speed for money.
Don't think for one second you can beat them.

In the park, you can safely listen at 2 am
(even if you're a bit drunk)
to musicians jamming heart-stopping music,
sharing your wine with friendly, exuberant
homeless people, almost none of them white.
You can walk where Bob Dylan and the late Suze Rotolo
walked for *Freewheelin' Bob Dylan*.

Be at Stonewall and remember.

Wander down MacDougal Street, in the footsteps of Woody
Guthrie, Huddy Ledbetter, Eugene O'Neill, Jack Kerouac,
Emma Goldman, James Baldwin, Paul Robeson, Miles Davis,
Dave Van Ronk, Joan Baez, Lawrence Ferlinghetti…

*****

When Greenwich Village was still something extraordinary, we
political freak-type multi-racial people trying
to live in a new way
used to yell out,
passing the women's prison
demolished now,

on 6th Avenue.
Calling loudly in solidarity to the women prisoners.

And they would wait and wait and listen for us all
and then call back,
their voices scraping, excited, above the traffic.

III

Homage:
If you stand among the artists and edgy bohemians
of Stanton Street, Clinton, Rivington,
and listen with your inner heart,
you can still hear whispers
of keening
where the waves of crammed-in immigrants
-- Jewish, Irish, German, Italian –
worked and wept and struggled.

Clutched dying children, often, in the cold,
amid the rats of the Lower East Side.

And longed, in stabbing disillusion perhaps,
for the fabled promise to begin.
Thousands already dead
on the crossing ships
that made money from famine and pograms.
They weren't called coffin ships for nothing.

Too bleak a picture?   Well, perhaps.

For many, it worked out eventually.
Brutal persecution left behind,
'new country' generations
moving to the suburbs,

all the sons and daughters going to college.

And the great Jewish organisations,
cultural, musical, political, social,
that people made…
the Irish societies, politics and dances…
All that self organising,
built out of poverty and immigration,
throughout the Lower East Side.

Forty five per cent of New Yorkers still live in,
or close to, poverty.
But
*'Give me your tired, your poor, your huddled masses
yearning to breathe free…'*
the great city
invited and invites…

IV

Homage:
People in midtown
-- even New Yorkers –
can't help staring at the Chrysler Building,
Art Deco masterpiece,
tallest in the world for just 11 months.

An upstart new skyscraper
named the Empire State
came fast on its heels,
winning the very public race
to become the great symbol of New York.
It was massively over-engineered,
you might be pleased to hear.

Desperate workers flocked
to fight for jobs on the work gangs.
It was the start of the Depression.
Three thousand four hundred employed on site,
the Kahnawake Mohawk Indians
journeying from Québec
to do the high welding.

It was a heartless schedule.
Hard to believe,
but the Empire State Building,
most famous of all modern buildings in the world --
even now --
went up at four and a half floors per week.

V

Homage:
The Dutch days still resonate downtown.
They built their protective wall
against the Native peoples who lived there.
Wall Street it's called now.

*****

The original governor, Peter Stuyvesant,
made his farm,
his Dutch 'Bouverie',
north of the settlement.

It became the Bowery,
infamous--well in the past anyway,
the sour tang of fear.
Now it's been regenerated with
clubs and on-trend bars.

The old broken alcoholics lying
across the sidewalks in mouldering heaps
have been kicked out.

(Where were they pushed to, you might wonder.
Are they in prison? Dead?
Lying on other streets far from Manhattan?
A dark joke told by New York progressives
during Mayor Giuliani's harsh clean-up period
imagined a deep hole dug in Queens,
into which the people were mowed.)

*****

At the other end of the island,
they made a village, the Dutch,
named it after their fine town of Haarlem.
You can whoosh up there on the subway,
the A Express,
built (people only half-joke)
to get black people in and out of midtown quickly.
Think Duke Ellington.
Just "Take the A Train."

Now, the statue of Harriet Tubman
pulling up the roots of slavery,
amid living cotton plants,
stands in a Harlem square,
when she should be feted downtown too,
as well as on these old streets.

These streets of the 1930s Harlem Renaissance,
Zora Neale Hurston, Langston Hughes....
blues and the jazz age too,
making unprecedented

African-American cultural transformations
in tough NYC.

VI

Homage:
New York, New York.
The original indigenous people
lost out big time,

pushed from their homeland,
decimated by smallpox,
forcibly moved en masse
thousands of miles away.

Not much compensation --
but the island was named
in the language of the Lenape Indians,
'Manna-hata',
'Island of many hills'.
Call it guilt, if you like.

It was bastardised into
Manhattan.

*****

But now the land they lost
is the great city of cities,
battered by 9/11,
but always boxing way above its weight.

It's no accident that the United Nations,
aiming to represent the whole world,
sits on the Upper East Side.

Or that people from everywhere come here,
rubbing along, often so bravely.

People from Korea, Dominican Republic, China, Iran,
from Puerto Rico, Afghanistan, Latvia, Yemen,

every one of them striving to survive,
carrying their memories, cultures, traditions.

Apparently, 800 languages are spoken in New York,
more than any other city.

And more new types of music,
new songs, new art,
more unfettered possibilities than in almost any other,
this city of cities,
that holds the dreams and desires
of people across the world.

An illiterate woman in a remote Moroccan village
clutched my arm hard, with eyes like gimlets,
"take me to New York, take me, take me."

(and a story)

A story: In a peeling New York deli, I sat among the poor, among Latinos, African-Americans. An old black man, full of welcome and friendliness to all-comers, waved in new people while addressing everyone loudly. In a heart-tearing way, he shouted his poetic words, as we all stoically ignored him and ate our bagels (though the young Puerto Rican guys at the back were jumping around to headphones, drinking out of bottles in brown bags). Without ever stopping, he sobbed and shouted slowly to the musty air, with choking gasps between the words. I wrote it down:

"America takes the dreams of the world. All over the world, we long for America. And then it sucks us in and then, it takes our dreams. And then, after it takes our dreams, it takes our blood. It sucks our hearts and spits us out..."

Sitting at a stained table in split shoes and torn trousers, with sores on his ankles, his eyes kept filling up with tears and a desperate human urgency to try to warn others - same words, over and over and over.

A frontier Old West graveyard and babies

Extracted from the gravestones of one old and isolated New Mexican frontier graveyard and from records recovered from this and one other.

An Old West graveyard from the Spanish / Mexican days,
as New Mexico became part of the Unites States.
There are signs everywhere
of the struggle just to keep living,
a hard, far place,
wind and sand churning across
the flat lands, el llano.
Only a couple of hundred are buried here,
leaving their mark
over all these years.
Almost no one lived past 50.

We'd been told of the Wild West days,
a saloon in the next isolated place across the desert plain,
tough single men trying to make a go of it.
But we don't see those graves,
rather they are families, wives, husbands, children.

There's a grave for one, Carolina.
The records tell us she grew up in Italy.
She had left the vines and sun to travel
alone,
surely intrepid,
crossing the ocean.

Then, the long daring trek
alone,
across the dangerous continent
to join her brothers in Albuquerque.

Then, she married their friend
and moved to this lonely settlement.
Then, possibly in childbirth or of disease,
she died.

She was 20.

II

Everyone's age at death is recorded
in days as well as years,
40 years, 25 weeks and 3 days,
says one gravestone.
Each day counts.

A shock,
although it shouldn't have been,
to see all the babies.
There probably wasn't a doctor.

A girl baby, Maria Doloritias, lived from
April 1886 till July 1886,
her sister, Ariana,
November 1888 till August 1889.

In one family,
Manuela, died 1887 aged 4 years,
Gregorio, died 1889 aged 8 years,
Rosaldo, died 1889, 4 months.
There was one long lived matriarch in that family, though.
Trinidad, 1828 - 1929.
Impossible to imagine what she must
have seen and known...

In another family grave,

Juanito, born 1889, died 1900.
Then Juanito, born 1900, died 1901,
buried together with a twin headed stone
shaped like two hearts.

Then Pedro, born 1902, died 1903.

They probably had other children.

But it seems they had a late try,
with sweet baby Josefita,
born 1912,
died 1912.

OK, so it's not simple...
Native Americans and Santa Fe (New Mexico): a prose poem

(In 1983, at the age of 96 after living for 40 years in New Mexico, Georgia O'Keeffe, the great American modernist painter, reflected that the crosses everywhere were "like the thin dark veil of the Catholic Church covering the New Mexico landscape."[9])

OK, so it's not simple...

Santa Fe: a mosaic of art, sculpture, beautiful things to look at everywhere you turn.

Its good-hearted people are mainly doing their best, organising environmental projects and non-profit theatres, running weekly blues jams, fantastic farmers markets. They are keen to celebrate the Latino and Native Indian history of this vast place. Terracotta adobe and turquoise are everywhere, shining colours in the dry thin air. The skies are too huge to countenance.

Downtown is like an art exhibition though -- you can't buy much useful, like screwdrivers or teabags, round here.

II

But it's enchanting, this little city, with its fiestas, international festivals, museums honouring all the local cultures. Men wear Stetsons and lots of people dance – the two-step anyway.

---

9   O'Keeffe, Georgia, words from 1976, Georgia O'Keeffe Museum, Santa Fe.

Outdoor concerts every night in summer, Latino bands, women's choirs, good-old-boy country singers with big grey beards and pony-tails, the world-renowned opera house under the stars. Huevos rancheros, enchiladas, margaritas, guacamole made often at your table, chiles always.

The New Mexico State Saying, asked by servers at every meal, pays homage to those chiles (not chillies):
"red or green?"

III

Here in Santa Fe, high-end Native Indigenous art gleams from the stores, 99% of them owned by whites. Sympathetic probably, but in business nonetheless. Several, for example, say that they sell precious-gemmed silver jewelry, possibly of ceremonial importance, for many hundreds, if not thousands, of dollars. It was harvested from the old reservation pawn shops.

Meanwhile, opposite the elegant stores, it's an uneasy thing to see that present day Indians from the Pueblos[10] are sitting daily in a long line on blankets and folding chairs trying to sell their jewelry, laid out on the ground. They sell expensively though. We are told they make enough money to survive, just about.

IV

In the Pueblo Revolt in 1680, after years of vicious treatment, the native people attacked the invading forces of Spain and drove them unceremoniously out.

---

10   The Pueblos are stable, respected Native American communities in New Mexico (now reservations), based on land they have always owned over centuries.

When the Pueblos were defeated again, 12 years later, the returning Spanish had learned, the story goes. The soldiers and padres could no longer impose their missions – well, not as much anyway. Apparently, there was less naked brutality.

But then the records show that, in the 1700s and 1800s, Indians were regularly abducted from the Pueblos by force to be lifelong domestic slaves. Those from both the Pueblos and the nomadic tribes,[11] who were captured attacking the Spanish settlements, were tightly chained to each other.

Then, they were marched for 2000 miles to be labouring slaves in Mexico City -- without ever once undoing the chains. (We could close our eyes and imagine the reality of such a journey.)

Later, they were marched to the coast instead, and transported to Cuba -- because they kept escaping in Mexico.

And walking the 2000 miles back home.

V

It was better than before, though, the books suggest. Really.

It's said the Pueblo and Spanish/Mexican peoples helped each other against incursions by hostile tribes. There was much cross-marriage. The different cultures blended in some places to produce new types of pottery, new music, fiestas, the Spanish/Pueblo Indian architecture style. The Pueblos became and remain proud and independent. Some have giant profit-making (sometimes) casinos.

---

11   Including, for example, the Navaho (the Diné), the various Apache groups (the Ndé), the Comanche and the Ute nations.

More: the Santa Fe Convention Center now names all its halls for the Pueblos, holds 'Native Treasures' events where Indigenous artists win awards, sell their work for many hundreds of dollars. I admire a necklace for $1800. My daughter studied in New Mexico's leading university, taking high-quality courses run by top Native American lecturers.

At Indian Market every year in Santa Fe, there are 1000 stalls selling Indigenous artwork. There are superb Grammy-winning Native musicians, and sometimes sparkling Indian break-dancing and hip-hop, like any other hip-hop – except that it honours the Ancestors.

OK, so it's not simple…

VI

But how can it be, then, in this land of opportunity, that you can still easily see the small brown housing units in the Pueblos, the impoverishment, the falling-apart cars, the drinking of too much cheap alcohol (including on officially dry reservations), the aching with broken dreams?

It is unfair to blame pretty Santa Fe for the injustices. If it can, it tries to right the wrongs -- (probably? maybe?). But actually it can't.

And neither can anybody, it looks like. Not so far, anyway.

VII

When the Spanish first set up missions here in the 1500s/1600s, Indian men who resisted or tried to pursue their own religions had one foot chopped off.

The soldiers, acting for the Church, would burst onto the Pueblos, raid the sacred Kivas, burn the ceremonial treasures, revered symbols for the worship of the earth.

They would whip the honoured priestly leaders, or hang them to death in the Pueblo plazas before the eyes of their own people.

Some tell how caciques, ancient chiefs, who watched the skies for the people of the Pueblos, were burned alive at the stake in the great Plaza of Santa Fe itself.

VIII

The nightmares are always close by. In the 1920s, for example, a whole Pueblo nation near Santa Fe, the Tesuque, closed its entry points and tried to starve itself to death, including the children, in protest at a new US government bill of the time.[12]

There is the odd darkly humorous moment. At Española, there is a statue of Oñate, the Conquistador who sawed off the right foot of the men of Acoma Pueblo. On the 400th anniversary of Oñate's Spanish Conquest, a group of Indian men secretly sawed off the statue's right foot.

---

12   The Bursum Bill would have allowed Pueblo land to be claimed by, or sold off to, whites and would have left the Pueblos unprotected. The bill was eventually defeated through the first-ever campaign by Native peoples that had the additional weight of famous white artists and activists behind it. It brought all the Pueblos together, the first time since the Pueblo Revolt.

The news reached Acoma, a hundred miles away in minutes, to universal jubilation. They left a note ending: 'Fair's fair'.

IX

Now, the government provides housing and welfare. White people are invited to attend Pueblo feast days providing they are respectful, turn off their cell phones, don't take photos. Native American horse experts get parts in big movies filmed locally. Pueblo schools have programmes. They're trying – (probably? maybe?)

OK, so it's not simple...

The official records don't play the game though. They say the drop-out rate for Pueblo school students, if they speak a Native language at home, is more than forty per cent.

Forty per cent.

X

We learned -- a privilege -- from an artist of the Jicarilla Apache Nation,[13] at the federally-funded Institute of American Indian Arts. She explained in clear aching text and image that children from her people, who were forcibly removed into Indian residential schools, wore military-style uniforms. It was not that long ago. It made them look identical, complete with army peaked caps.

She reproduced a photo. You'd never have known they weren't military cadets.

13   The Jicarilla Apache nation is sited in an area of New Mexico north of the Pueblos.

Every single time they spoke their language, they were forced to eat lye soap. Since, she said, they could not speak English, they did not speak at all.

*****

The artist states that she yearns to see a time when: "my people are sober, liberated, healed."

Used with the agreement of the artist, Judith Vicenti, a studio and fine arts graduate from the Institute of American Indian Arts. Her piece was exhibited in the Museum of Contemporary Native Arts, Santa Fe, and is called "What will you wear to the Post-Colonial Trauma Disorder Reconstruction Party."

She can be contacted at walkingbadger@gmail.com.

Jaisalmer Days

Jaisalmer is in the North-Western State of Rajasthan near the Pakistan border.

It's early morning

It's early morning,
air like pearls.
All the young men who work at the hotel
are asleep on the flat roof
or illicitly watching the TV,
left out in the open air
by the boss's family, the night before.

On the street at this early hour,
the auto-rickshaw drivers don't bother to harass us.
"Sir, where are you going?"
"Tuc-tuc, madam, where to? Where are you from?"
the much-used joke:
"Try my Ferrari, look it's air-conditioned"
and always then a laugh.

Instead, they are transporting bevies of children
to school, waved off by proud parents
standing amid crushed paper-cups
at the chai stall.

Men are sitting cross-legged on the side of the road,
leaning forward,
eagerly reading yesterday's paper,
brought in by fast driving cars
to this desert outpost.

Cows wander by
looking philosophical and distant,
rather dirt-encrusted,
and packs of flea-bitten dogs snarl
and jump nervously,
but could gang up and turn nasty at any moment.
Some of them shake and twitch,
pariah dogs all,
not like the hotel owners' pampered dachshunds.

The boss's wife looks young
but regal like her husband,
recognisably of Rajput stock.
She is a modern woman clearly
with her laptop and smart-phone.
She talks down to us in educated English.
We never see her leave the haveli's walls though.

In the morning light, she reads the Baghavad Gita
looking serene and still by the fountain,
as her Maharani forbears probably also did.
But at night on the roof
with her family around her,
we see her watching bad-quality,
imported American TV.

Hard to have royal blood

They have long eyelashes,
these men who are almost royals.
Some of them were educated at Oxford.

They've hit hard times these days.

It's said they are relatives of
the Maharaja of Jaisalmer,
with their pale skins,
big black moustaches,
hawk eyes sometimes,
looking down long noses
at the young white tourists.
They don't smile often.

They come from a long heraldic line
of warrior kings
fiercely protecting their desert fort.

In the fifteenth century,
some of them, facing certain defeat,
slashed the throats of their own wives and children
in mass suicide johars

before riding proud
to their own inevitable deaths.

II

They were bound by networks of hierarchy,
honour -- still are, partly --
duty beyond any Western understanding.

They're not keen on sharing their wealth though.

The post-Independence Nehru government
duped them all.
Now they have to run hotels
and museums that charge-for-entry
in their palaces,
put up with loud Westerners
staying in their great carved havelis,
taking their newspapers just as they were
about to read them,
leaving on the air-conditioning full-blast.

Common Westerners who wander round
their gorgeous private courtyards
in shorts and skinny t-shirts,
and shout to each other
in crude American and UK accents,
disrupting moments of traditional serenity,
not understanding about hierarchy and nobility,
or how to behave in royal company,
worse, not caring.

It's hard to have royal blood these days

Luckily for them, at any time of day or night,
they can still jerk their chins,
condescending and unsmiling,
and order the servants about,
who everyone still calls 'boys'.

Jaisalmer, tradition, women and tourists

You don't see these men
of Rajasthan
walking round
with bare legs and chests,
wearing a dhoti on its own,
like the brown-skinned guys in Kerala
often do.
Bound by tradition,
you couldn't get them to even countenance it.

On the road, their Hindu wives have their faces
completely covered
in bright coloured muslin.
The shape of their noses is all that shows through.
After marriage,
no other man but their husband can see them.

Mind you, when one woman gestures to us
to take a picture of her flute-playing children,
she whips up her veil pretty damn quick
to see the digital photo.

II

A children's troupe bounces cheerfully
from hotel terrace to terrace,
singing traditional songs
with sprightly gusto
and years of (quite possibly harsh) study.
They are doing it for the young Western travellers

who of course are totally ignorant

about the whole thing,
but properly enthusiastic,
worrying if they are clapping in the right places
and how much is the right amount to tip.

III

Still, in 42 degree dryness,
the roof top restaurants sparkle
under the flood-lit fort and starry desert sky,
the Maharaja's palace the highest roof of all,
overlooking all of gilded Jaisalmer.

Overlooking the wind masts too,
that apparently serve the armed forces.
From here, it is just 100 kilometres to Pakistan
and the closed dangerous border.
No one can go any closer than here.
Fighter planes zap by daily.
It wasn't meant to have turned out like this.

India's nuclear bombs were tried out
just down the road too.
We are told a whole group of tribal people
arrived later
with unknown illnesses.

IV

In the desert, there is no work at all.
Too dry to grow anything.
Too remote these days to trade.
Even the camel drivers on the holiday safaris
seem to get almost nothing.
The tourist dollars

are few and far between, they say,
and the camel owners take them.

But there is a University here
and there has been a tripling of male literacy --
it's still just 25% for women.

V

The golden mediaeval fort
stands as in an ancient myth
of chivalry and princes.
It looks like a row of sand castles,
though its history is one of gore and blood.
Bits of it are subsiding now.
It is one of the most threatened
Heritage sites in the world.

Today, though, it is shimmering yellow
in the great heat
that lies on you like a blanket,
choking the air as you try to breath it.

Stone-laced carving
of stunning intricacy,
Jain temples, quietly non-violent
in this fierce place.
You can't go in with leather shoes
or if you are menstruating.
(We are told it's a trust system.)

VI

The story goes that
the Rajputs protected

the deeply religious Jains,
the honest traders,
who grew prosperous.

Our guide tells us
how poor he is in contrast.
He has glowing yogic eyes
and meditates two hours, twice a day.
He says it is essential if you are to survive.

Somewhat confusingly, he wears a traditional
silk coat and turban
as did the Rajput nobles of old.
Later we are shocked when we see him,
in ordinary clothes
looking like everyone else.

VII

The colours of the tribal women's costumes
hurt the eyes in this brilliant light.
Gathered ghagra skirts they wear,
their veils pushed back,
and giant noisy anklets of metal.
Their eyes sparkle
although you can scarcely imagine why.
Their lives are too harsh
for Western visitors to contemplate,
as they sell
two,
no, four,
no, six,
no, all right, I give you ten

silver bracelet chains
for a dollar,
and grubby babies cling to their hips.

VIII

There can be a franticness in the air,
a scrabbling for the tourist's money.

This noble Silk Route city,
legendary on the great journey
of spices, silks and gold.
Now the precious brocades and gems
go by sea or air.

The final nail came at Partition.

It's stranded,
marooned against a desolate no-man's-land,
its life line cut forever.

How then can such a stately town,
drenched in history and blood
and old merchant etiquette,
survive?

Now, it has porters fighting over passengers
from the only bus
(our bag was wrenched apart and left in pieces),
Indian air-force planes streaking past,
lost pauper boys from desert villages

and clamouring hustlers
with the sharp light of desperation
haunting their eyes.

Havana, Cuba

Written on a study trip and vacation.
Note: this poem was written in 2012.

A vertical learning curve

Cuba.
A vertical learning curve for us
-- with the help of mohitos and cuba libres.
Possibly unwisely, we think,
the people over there
are on their third.

At night, there is a straightforward side.
Maybe it's because of the great revolución.
(No gang warfare here,
people are surprised when we tell them
about street crime. "What's that," they say.)

But it's also maybe
because of the vibrant
good humour, the rum.

II

Music jumps from every corner,
the venerable 'Son' of Cuba,
the Cha Cha,
the African Rhumba.

The musicians are vivacious,
never stop moving.

The sexy glide and step of the Cuban salsa.
It's not the same as salsa anywhere else.
Seems everyone here can do it.
They teach you at school.

Looking earnestly into our eyes,
a local friend explains
the clean impossibility of visitors learning it,
despite valiant trying.

III

The famed revolución goes on.
Yet, hopes get stalled, we're told.
The materials the society needs
are stopped by the blockade,
even now after all these years and reforms.

It's been like a stranglehold,
more –
a total strangling.

Eager, ground-breaking
Revolución de Cuba.

How much chance have you had?

IV

On the other hand,
there are services and welfare for all,
new art enterprises and cell phones,
a gorgeous architecture,
masterfully restored UNESCO squares
(despite the mighty Malecón

crumbling now along the bay).
Things are changing for sure.
Fidel still gives some speeches
but his brother is in charge.
There's a whole new team coming up,
none of them named Castro.

Fidel commands huge respect though.
Everyone uses his first name.
A motorcycle-taxi driver, strongly dissident
and against the government as too left-wing,
tells us sagely:
"He's a thinking man."

He's also seen off 10 American presidents.

V

We stay with a gay guy in the country
and meet his wildly extrovert friends.
They make us feel staid and boring.
We make an effort not to be.

The bad times are long gone, he tells us.
His lesbian sisters, his lovers,
they can all be proud, he says.

Now there are African-Cuban LGBT groups
(a bit clandestine still, but they exist).

We join him at a lively dance at a village bar
in the open air.
All his young friends
hug each other extravagantly.

VI

Back in the city, we see heart-rending scenes
at the airport
as people in tears are wrenched apart,
sobbing hopelessly,
trying to cling to their loved ones,
their Miami-Cuban relatives,
leaving to go home again.

A man tells us that
you are best only saying
what you think
if it agrees with the Government.

Others say those days have passed
when you had to keep an eye out for the
Comités de Defensa de la Revolución.

They're there on every street though.
(We're assured they do good neighbourhood work, too.)

VII

We see plenty of antique Soviet tractors
still tilling the land.

When Soviet support ended
and the 'Special Period' began,
people nearly starved.
Some ate insects, an émigré friend tells us.
The Russian stores,
the 'red markets', had to close.

Now the black markets are everywhere

(at least, here, en Habana).

The CUC[14] is king, the new king.
Everyone wants some.

A man asks us: "you want to eat, my friends,
here is my restaurant."
"You want a casa particular?"[15]

People come rushing up,
offering taxis, cervesas,
hand-made cigars,
tours in pink 1950s American cars,

or small-scale hustles
where you get to pose with someone
dressed as a traditional Cuban stereotype,
or someone else asks you to laugh
for money at a dog
in sun-glasses, hat and cigar…

VIII

A woman offers us a 3 peso coin,
almost worthless,
but the one with the famous picture of Che,
the best known image the world over, apparently.
Che turns in his grave.

14   The CUC, the Convertible Cuban Peso is the currency used for tourists and some
businesses. It is highly desirable and worth about 24 times the other currency, used by the
people, known as the Peso or Cuban Peso.
15   A 'casa particular' is someone's house where tourists can rent rooms and stay as
guests of the occupants.

It's commercially exploited everywhere --
except here.

She gives the special coin genuinely.
"Please take it home as a memory of Cuba," she tells us
(which we will do and show it proudly).
But then, of course,
she wants a CUC or two, instead.
We respond, obviously.

IX

Another woman says to us: "look at it."
"Look at the yoke the people have to carry.
It has to change, it has to."

But many others point to
free education
free healthcare
(almost) free housing for all
camp holidays, food security
free university, free books
free doctors
free medicines, great auto-pistas
free operations
dedicated environmental projects run by campesinos
no advertising whatsoever
exercise programmes for the children.

We are amazed at these healthy children,
erupting out of school,
loud, laughing, glowing.

A country can't be doing too badly
if its children look like this,

far healthier than across the Florida Strait.

X

Late last night, the hotel guys were watching
American baseball on TV.

Now, it's volleyball.
A huge match,
Cuba against Italy.

All over the city,
people watch noisily
in small dark living rooms
with an open door to the hot street,
sitting in front of tiny TVs
on plastic chairs
or on cheaply tapestried sofas
with lace, and photos on the side
of Fidel
or their loved ones
or sometimes the Virgin.

People watching too
in rocking chairs on balconies
staring into scruffy box-like 60s apartments
built to solve the housing shortage.

Waiters in bars lean on their elbows,
their eyes fixed to the screen
ignoring customers.
Crowds peer into hot stained cafes…

Cheering erupts in the dark streets
as Cuba wins hands down.

Five hundred gringos and a love long gone

They were going to Mexico
travelling through the Deep South,
white woman, black man.
It was 1969.
They'd been shoved hard off the sidewalk,
spat at,
gobs of mucus.

He wouldn't leave the Greyhound bus-station after that.
She saw the Southern Hate Stare first-hand.
The usual foul, unrepeatable insults
bored into her ears.
She ran, icy with fear in the heat.
Somehow, she'd thought,
with her white entitlement,
the police would help her.
They wouldn't.

In Mexico,
people passing by
knew about that stuff,
remembered the signs: 'No Blacks. No Mexicans.'

They rushed up to hug him on the street,
called him their brother.

She was proud with love.

They hitchhiked to Acapulco
where giant cockroaches sat on every post
(there had been a storm).
They decided it was retribution for unbridled tourism,
slept and laughed on the white beach.

It didn't last.
They stayed friends.
Now they are touching 70.

But in Mexico, at Teoteucan,
she would have given him
the Pyramid of the Sun,
del Sol,
except there were
five hundred gringos standing on it.

A Villanelle for exiled Latin American revolutionaries in Mexico City

From time to time, Mexico City acts as a sanctuary for revolutionaries and left-wing activists exiled or expelled from other Latin American countries. They may have experienced imprisonment, torture and brutality.

Here, the rhyming villanelle is used in an attempt to accentuate the contrast between its formal rules and both the seriousness and bravery of the exiled people involved who made up entirely new rules.

Tortured, pursued, driven from their countries,
they drank Cuban rum, tequila all night.
Far from home, these revolutionaries.

They'd found haven in this best of cities,
talked politics always, bruised in their fight.
Tortured, pursued, driven from their countries.

Smoked dope, gave fiestas, danced, ate tamales,
laughed in Chapultepec Park in the light.
Far from home, these revolutionaries.

Met black ex-soldiers on GI Bill fees,
strung out by Vietnam, sick at US might.
Tortured, pursued, driven from their countries.

Shared traumatic stories, feeling at ease.
Dissidents all, they clung together tight.
Far from home, these revolutionaries.

Partied together, made frail families,
longed for their mothers, scarred deep by their flight.
Tortured, pursued, driven from their countries.

Racked by the 'disappeared', the memories,
twisting, trying in their pain and their right.
Tortured, pursued, driven from their countries.
Far from home, these revolutionaries.

Andalucia, Spain

Even so, we love you, Frigiliana

"Granada was the last Spanish kingdom where mosques, churches and synagogues could live side by side in peace," suggests the late Eduardo Galeano in *Children of the Days: A Calendar of Human History*.[16]

This is his entry for January 2nd, the day Granada fell in 1492.

After 800 years, the Islamic Moors lost out in Spain,
finally defeated in Granada in 1492.
A hundred years later, the remaining Moriscos,
hounded, scourged, forcibly converted to Christianity,
fought a last bitter battle here

in the Andalucian mountains.
At the end, both men and women raced to leap
en masse from this great secluded cliff.
They would not surrender.
The forces of the Spanish King drove them over.

There were screams perhaps,
bodies twisting as they fell.
You can imagine the shattered bone and
blood and brain matter.
Just like mine or yours would be.

Now, the international visitors
pay little attention or aren't told.
They buy Frigiliana honey

16   Galeano, Eduardo (2013) *Children of the Days: A Calendar of Human History*, New York: Nation Books.

and happily eat tapas
and patatas a lo pobre.

But this is the very edge of Fortress Europe.
Descendants of the Moors and Moriscos
trying to cross the Mediterranean
are blocked at entry,
imprisoned, deported, drowned.

Some Moroccans working here legally
in the poly-tunnels
talk quietly about the brutal entry process,
barbed wire border fences,
the guns with rubber bullets at Ceuta.

This is never brought to tourist eyes either.

Rock on, sweet Malta

Seems like the Fifties but everyone has an iPhone

There were little ironmongers
(owned by Joe Spinioli
or the Il-Ahmarq brothers)
with 1950s-type window displays
of piles of boxes with their products still in them.
But everyone had iPhones.

There were global chain-stores too,
just as in the UK,
with the very same sales on.
Boots, Next, Marks and Spencer's,
among the one-off businesses with
folding metal shutters
like the doors on antique lifts.

It all felt a bit off kilter.
This rocky, tiny island of stone walls,
rough ground, pre-historic remains, tourist trips.
Guys on the promenade quickly
started to recognise us.
They followed us daily
with repeated offers of 'three harbours' cruises,
a hop-on hop-off bus.
"Here you are again. Are you from the UK?"
"Which hotel are you in? I will pick you up."
(Best not to tell them,
perhaps.)

II

Just 500,000 people here altogether,
speaking their fine language,
Arabic but Italian,
written in Roman script.
No-one else can understand it.

They raced across roads to be of assistance,
"Do you need some help?"
"Do this. No, not that way."
They were definite and forthright, in the main.

And what a people.

They've withstood more sieges
than anyone else in history,
from Suleiman the Magnificent and the Ottoman Empire
to fascist besiegement by the Mussolini navy
and Nazi bombardment.

Malta, fortified to excess
by the Knights of Saint John
and by everyone else,
including the Brits.

Poor people,
their tiny island,
a strategic lynchpin
that the Empires of the world have coveted
and endlessly fought over.

The Phoenicians, the Carthaginians,
the Romans, the Arabs,

the Spanish, the Ottomans,
the Italians, the French,
the British...

Intimidating sand-brown forts
and colossal walls guard the cities.
Now the Grand Harbour is peaceful,
except that, in direct accord with the Empire issue,
a huge US warship sits there silently, waiting.

Just in case.

III

They hold the George Cross,
these people, this island.

For unprecedented valour
under siege to almost-starvation,
interminable bombing
in the Second World War.

The George Cross.
The only island or whole people to be so honoured.
And they put it proudly
on their now republican flag.

IV

The young people don't seem bothered
about all that, though.
They are smart and loud.
Everyone in suave wrap-around sunglasses in the winter,
teamed with leather jackets and stylish scarves,
drinking beers or tiny espressos,

smoking as a matter of course (but with panache).

In summer, on the other hand,
it is about 40 degrees.

Rabbit is on all menus
and circular pies full just of peas.
There are some sweet ones too
filled with dates.
On the radio, there's hip hop in Maltese.

The architecture is often heavy baroque,
great fortified Catholic buildings
weighing down oppressively on the land.
On human freedom too, one would guess.
In the past, anyway.

At Marsaxlokk,
the old fishing harbour is full of
painted fishing boats,
in bright, contrasting colours and traditional patterns.

Every single one has the eye of Osiris,
ancient Phoenician god,
on the bow,
to ward off shipwreck out at sea.
An unbroken tradition for, what,
4000 years?

Rock on, sweet Malta.

Malta by car hire

The places here have names like
Wied Iz-Zurrieq,
Tarxien, Gudja,
Hal Ghazaq,
Hagar Qim,
to the bewilderment
of UK tourist drivers chasing the sun.

On top of the surprise of the
battered hire cars,
perhaps with outdated car-radios
held in by sellotape
and with so many things not working
that local musicians make up
satirical songs about them.

Luckily, though, nothing is further than
a few kilometres from anywhere else.
The central ancient city, Mdina, for instance.
It sits strategically on a hill,
within massive fortifications.
Golden Arabic-type passageways wind
in a medieval maze.

But you can get pizza there
and coloured Valetta glass
with ferocious patterns,
though no clear function often.
(Its swirling beauty is everything.)
The parades and festivals, with fireworks,
are wildly coloured too.

There are carnival-cakes
built like bright studded towers,
pagan figures with bizarre faces
and local saints borne round
villages on shoulders.
Your hire car might get you there in summer.
Or you can take a bendy bus.

They roar round tight turns,
with the frequent danger
(usually avoided it seems)
of hitting something
as the back section whips past people strolling.
They only cost two Euros though
and will take you anywhere on the island.

Our car got a puncture on the splintered roads
(men rushed to help us change the tyre).
It had gears you had to ram with all your strength.
"Might be the clutch," the car-hire man shrugged
with a down-turned mouth and a knowing nod,
clearly with no intention
of doing anything about it.

Getting any money back
met a wall of resistance.

Shortly after, a bit of the car fell off the side.
Yes, rock on, sweet Malta.

It's good to know that...

It's good to know when you come back
after being in other countries
where you can't do these things
that...

You can get welfare benefits
(even if currently under fierce government attack)
You can go to the doctor without paying (ditto)
Stays in hospital are free (ditto)
You can go to a public library (ditto)
There's still some public sector housing (ditto)
You can watch incisive documentaries
on Channel 4 or the BBC
(try this in the Southern US...).

It's good to know when you come back
that...

This country has spawned organisations like
Oxfam, Amnesty, Liberty
There are 400 year old buildings and ancient oak trees
Blackbirds sing on the roof tops at sunset
You can see young people take over the city centres
on Saturday night, trying to get fall-down drunk,
well, not just trying...
(What? Most of them turn out fine.)

It's good to know when you come back
that…

You are in a place with a venerable tradition of
radical protest,
from the Diggers to the Suffragettes to the Match Girls,
from the Miners' Strike to women's liberation
Where millions will demonstrate against war
(even if they are then ignored)
Where diversity is in the city air
Where there is at least some attempt
at multi-culturalism

Where there are ancient country footpaths
free to the public
Where being an island
can give a strange and sea-bound feel
Where wild cliffs surround our coasts
Where no one owns the beaches
Where you can enjoy the Spring,
first crocuses, snowdrops, pale-bright leaves,
this bursting northern Spring,
new birdsong and daffodils everywhere,
acknowledged by that old BBC itself
as one of the wonders of the world.

These poems expand on, and relate closely back to, the previous tribute to Mifumi in Uganda. The poem below is about Mifumi Primary School, set up where previously there were no schools or education available.

MIFUMI P/S

In bright yellow uniforms,
they run laughing to meet us,
jarring to a halt at the last minute.
They giggle, covering their mouths.
Their eyes follow us.

One hundred and eight children jammed in,
we count inside one classroom,
squeezed into twelve rows of nine,
elbow to elbow.
Each with an old pencil
and one ripped notebook.

All they've ever had,
they painstakingly copy out their work,
hand-drawn charts
all round the wall.
They learn more than most of us
in the West
could possibly answer
without a machine to help us.

Fourteen times fourteen,
the parts of an ear,
four-figure long division.

Five to ten miles they walk, each way,
just to get here,
these children,
sometimes without breakfast.
Always a mug of porridge at lunch-time.
They are intent to study hard
all of every long day.

They say they want to be doctors or lawyers,
professors they are less convinced about.

They don't yet realise
how hard life is likely to be,
but maybe not for all,
maybe not for all.

They glow and shine
in the soaking heat of their unique school
which says that education can fix all this,
holds fast to the beacon of learning,
teaches girls of twelve to resist early marriage,
boys to respect their later wives.

This strong school of theirs,
it battles for enough funding,
but it stands firm on its own green land,
helped by people from here and overseas.

Let us raise our hands and affirm again
these joyous and bitter acts of challenge.

For the women

When I came to this luscious country,
I did not expect to meet
quite such rare and exceptional women.

Truly rare and exceptional
by any count, world-wide.
I have felt humbled indeed.

These are not the sophisticated, educated women
who run the NGO,
although they are astonishing too.

No, these women come from remote villages,
each one spread-out over miles.
Many do not read or write.

They live a subsistence life of poverty,
exactly where they always have.
They have become involved in fighting

domestic violence,
with deep, deep courage
beyond what I can even start to imagine.

They organise for women and children,
care for their own families,
stand up to opponents in their villages.

Often they are in danger,
having to take care in case
hostile individuals beat them up.

Some of them dare not buy food
from male traders locally
for fear of poisoning.

They spend their lives, these village women,
supporting other women
across their rural homeland,

living and breathing what they believe.
And what they believe is that they must stay strong
and help any woman in trouble,

give them some of that strength,
provide refuge and safety,
in the struggle against abuse by men.

*****

Yes,
across your districts,
you offer solace to those who come,

beaten, distressed, raped,
or with raped children, some with HIV,
rural women and children, desperate,

maybe with no possessions,
possibly on the edge of starvation.
But needing you all to stand firm with them.

And you always do
-- with police assistance
which cannot always be relied on.

(One sympathetic rural police station

has just one motorbike for a vast road-less area;
others are uninterested, sometimes oppositional.)

You stand strong at great risk to yourselves
to give some power to the women
and take some power from the men.

The men tend to do what they can to stop you.
This is gender equality work at its most testing.
'Power and control' work at its most clear.

'Power and control' that we endlessly speak about
in the domestic violence movements across the world,
but don't always practice.

You are doing it
without being able to read
any of the famous books.

*****

You are heroes indeed,
in the fight we are all engaged in
for women and against violence.

I've seen you.
As you care for ten extra children,
go bravely to talk with police bosses.

As you travel to remote places
to rescue women and children
who may have been violated horribly,

and take them into your homes
to share your food,

sleep in your one room.

As you go with them to hospital,
shield them at the door
if the men come,

sit some of these men down
and give them
a stern talking-to,

organise singings,
speak-outs,
outdoor celebrations,

give ululations of joy.

To Jane-Rose and Immaculate, the respected elders of the activists, among so many

Note: Jane-Rose and Immaculate are the elders or respected seniors among the village activists. They work on domestic violence advocacy in Mifumi's centres, endlessly supporting domestic violence survivors and their children. Over very many years, they have both carried out this work with total dedication, including all the activities mentioned above.

This tribute to Jane-Rose and Immaculate is included with the agreement of them both and of Mifumi.

Dear Jane-Rose and Immaculate. Thank you for agreeing to let me speak of you.

You are dedicated beyond belief. You live for women in your villages. And hundreds of women and children, if not thousands, have benefited from your committed, thorough, powerful work. Taking women in, finding them shelter, counselling and strengthening them, sharing everything you have with them, almost always putting yourselves last in order to help them in their crisis. Sometimes you are in danger. Activists on domestic violence in the UK and elsewhere could learn much from your courage and commitment and vision.

You have devoted your lives to abused women and children. What a gift and an inspiration indeed. Please know that you are heroes and beacons to all around you.

Thank you deeply from all of us who struggle to end domestic violence not only in Africa, but across the world.

In Kerala, gentle place

Well, there is religion everywhere you look,
despite an egalitarian
communist past that feels refreshing.
The Muslim call to prayer
floats on the heat from the minarets
and, in every nook and corner,

fat blue Krishnas with mischievous eyes dance.
There's a surfeit
of very white Christs,
against the dark skins
that these Southern people have and need.
Like Shiva, the Christs have jasmine garlands

and incense, but their hearts are
painted bright red, exposed
and tortured, dripping.
Hundreds crowd outside the churches
as the services are loud-speakered
across the whole neighbourhood.

There are adverts
for God's own estate agents
and Christ's second hand motors
where you can get your old car fixed.
There's also 98 percent literacy
and everyone goes to school.

Cherai, Aluwa

Being stared at, at all times,
and with drops of sweat between my eye-lashes,
I walk through
pulsing dusty towns

where the heat lies like treacle.
The men spend a lot of time
tying up their lungis
and then untying them.

And everything has coconut in it.
Yes, this is good country
where Ayurvedic philosophy
can caress you.

In this place of water and cardamoms,
a thousand coconut palm trees rustle
against a tropical sky,
but this idyll is environmentally threatened.[17]

We may not have it long.

17   In Kerala, environmental difficulties include precious backwaters disappearing,
choked waterways, the dredging of fragile canals, new rogue species of water-creepers
taking over, and both air and water pollution.

At Agape

A unique project for mental health survivors in Mamelodi Township near Pretoria. A version of this tribute poem was presented as a gift to Agape after the visit described here, and was received in that spirit.

And so, in the hard-faced township,
we went to Agape Healing Community,
a place of love.
A Greek word confusingly,
not Zulu or Xhosa.

Agape.
We found out later
that it had a Tswana word in it
meaning 'again'.
'Love again', and then
'Make it all again'.

*****

Agape.
A place where township
meets therapeutic mental health project
in a strange and unexpected mix.

And psychotherapy,
like the proverbial emperor,
has thrown away its protective clothes,
cast off all that therapy orthodoxy.

They refused their own building under apartheid
which would have imposed control
and attack, very likely,
preferring instead to meet in the open air.
They still do.

The idea is to construct
healing
without professional walls or places
to hide behind or within.

*****

At Agape,
the safe and quiet consulting room,
full of authority,
becomes a dusty corner in a rough yard,
or a patch of scruffy shade beneath the tree
with garbage along the fence.

Filing cabinets of confidential case notes,
locked in offices,
have become, in the words of one therapist:
"a file in the back of Stan's truck."

Efficient records though they are, for sure,
they might lie tangled up
with the drums.

*****

Women and men gather around.
Instead of going alone, isolated,
for a therapy session,
they share each other's hurt.

Outside, through the gate,
standing open to whoever wants to come,
the clamour of township life continues.
We are told of the bitterness of life here,
poverty, often violence,
despite some new post-apartheid housing.
"This is a very hard place",
say the project's pioneer leaders,
"recovering from a very hard history."

The people come bearing their pain and wounds.

*****

There is a low spiral wall,
peach-coloured, with graffiti,
where meetings are held
and everyone sits
to pass the carved Talking Stick
(in spirals, too)
four times a day.
Each person thinks and carefully speaks
when they receive it.

Some have been coming here
for ten years, week after week.

People wander around --
it all feels a little haphazard --
greeting, hugging, crying,
telling stories.
Loud drumming competes with the talking.

*****

A young girl
(her new name is 'Beauty'
and who is beautiful indeed)
keeps laughing,
after crippling mental health crises,
life and energy bursting out of her sorrow.

She speaks
so proudly of her transformation,
so proudly of her studies
in the township's University,
of her qualification (one-day, everyone hopes)
to become a "proper psychologist."
And, in her case,
a healer of the soul.

Another woman speaks
of the dark side, the terror.
A sangoma, a traditional healer, visits
and is honoured,
bringing ancient wisdom.

The chairwoman of the ANC Women's League
offers mature warmth and healing.
A public telephone sitting on a table at the roadside
has been set up by three members
who have donated their own welfare money for it.

The counselling session
becomes a swirl of people,
coming and leaving and drumming.
And looking into each others' eyes as they speak.

*****

There is a round open thatched area
where four women cook for everyone.
At lunch time, people crowd together,
women and men, elders and children.

Two girls sing and everybody listens.
Some people give speeches,
welcoming us who have come from afar.
Some bear witness.
Times have been hard, people tell.
A small graceful ritual of water and candles
is held to protect and heal us all.

We honour each other
before sharing food together
in that ancient way that humans do.

*****

One day there for us –
mother and early teenage son together,
coming from another country –
will be remembered always.
Thank you, Agape.

We understand little.
We are welcomed with generosity,
greeted over and over
by people who have nothing,
as if we are their family.

My son drums in the heat,
in the middle of the dusty expanse,
the only white person
in the music circle

among the huge African drums,
joining in with rather scary-looking expert drummers.
He bravely plays blues guitar too.

A disturbed man gives us his writing,
A young girl insists we take her poetry.

In the sharp sun, I am requested to be
with a women's group,
have to leave my son again to fend for himself.
We talk of abuse and loss,
of the gaping wounds of domestic violence,
of repeated sexual assaults and rape.
For some, if not all, the women,
this is the stuff of their lives most days.

They console each other
and warmly share with me.
I am humbled.

Later, we walk through the township streets to the store
(to everyone's interest),
escorted by people being helped
long-term by Agape,
hearing their savage stories
of hurt and the making of art.

Some people ask for money or cigarettes.

*****

We gather towards the end,
passing the Talking Stick for the last time,
with silences, soft and strong.
People contribute what they feel or can.

Some talk of wild, sad feelings,
some cry and speak of the agony of friends
raped as babies or as young children.

Some talk of days of birth and becoming --
it`s a member's birthday today.

Some talk of pleasure in our presence.

And unexpectedly, some talk
of butterflies.

*****

A post script:
On another of my visits alone,
a few years later,
the expert drummers remember my son
"Where is your wonderful son, the musician?"

That day, after some brief words together,
everyone agrees
and they leave an empty chair
in the Talking Stick circle for him.

When people make great symbols: I

The following two connected poems celebrate the South African Constitutional Court via Brasilia and Washington.

When people make great symbols,
we can maybe see
humanity at its best.

Leaps of faith.
Like Brasilia, designed from scratch
by the greatest modernist architects,

avant-garde,
futuristic at the time.
It looks a bit chipped these days.

Still, its symbolism shines.
From above, designed to look like
a flying bird or butterfly.

All the government ministries
exactly the same
to avoid one-upmanship.

The three buildings that trump them
are deliberately taller
in a huge U-shape,

the Executive and Legislature
facing each other,
linked by the third, highest of all,

to show through architecture

that it can over-ride all the others.
It's the Parliament of the People.

(On a towering flagstaff though,
the national flag hangs higher still
to make it clear that Brazil's sovereignty

must dominate all else –
chilling during the past days
of fascist military dictatorship.)

II

Or take Washington, DC.
Built on land given by Virginia and Maryland
so the brand new capital

would not be part of any State,
could not be ransomed to vested State interest.
The streets form an egalitarian grid,

just with numbers,
criss-crossed diagonally by the avenues,
named for each of the States.

The only real names saved for the
great emblematic boulevards,
Constitution, Independence…

That long 'Reflecting Pool'
the world sees on TV
perfectly fulfilling its task

to reflect the celebrated monuments.
Martin Luther King stood above it

to tell of his dream,

all the biggest demonstrations ending there,
Obama addressing the world,
claiming "Yes We Can" too soon.

The grand National Mall
reaches from the Lincoln Memorial
to the Washington Memorial obelisk,

no building in the city is allowed,
unofficially, to be higher.
On one side, the White House of course.

Tourists stare at it from the front
though the famous photos are of the back.
It's not as big

as people imagine.
No doubt as to its power though,
as victims of war after war can testify.

Washington, a leap of faith,
an inspired lay-out,
for something not tried before.

Oh, great experimental nation,
the new United States,
vehicle of a human dream,

what happened?

When people make great symbols: II

The new Constitution of South Africa, adopted in 1996, remains one of the most progressive in the world, inspiring millions, after the brutality of apartheid. It attempts to shape a new society with its progressive judgments, e.g. on violence against women, on banning capital punishment, on providing housing for the poor, and on gay and lesbian marriage. It is a beacon among African – in fact all – national constitutions (even if South Africa overall remains on an unsure path). A sensational modern Court Building was built in a low-income neighbourhood to house the Court and opened in 2004.

At the opening, Nelson Mandela said: "The Constitutional Court building will stand as a beacon of light, a symbol of hope and celebration. Transforming a notorious icon of repression into its opposite, it will ease the memories of suffering inflicted in the dark corners, cells and corridors of the Old Fort Prison. Rising from the ashes of that ghastly era, it will shine forth as a pledge for all time that South Africa will never return to that abyss. It will stand as an affirmation that South Africa is indeed a better place for all."

When people make great symbols,
we can maybe see
humanity at its best.

For the most symbolic of buildings,
let us look then towards
the Constitutional Court of the New South Africa.

This pale modern building
has its name on the outside
in all eleven official South African languages.

A place of light with walls of glass,
unlike other heavy court buildings.
One of the judges explains how

it aims to be transparent,
to make the Law transparent,
participant, accessible.

Anyone can walk in if they wish.
Trite to call it awe-inspiring,
but no other words will do.

The oppressive symbols of apartheid
destroyed by the architects to make instead
a symbol of new participatory values,

the Court's stated aim in fractured South Africa
is the dignity of human persons.
All of them.

II

The highest court in the land,
it stands proud
in an impoverished neighbourhood.

Constructed with bricks
from the old apartheid prison,
but now those bricks are slashed through

by vertical windows,
bringing great streams of light
into the previous dark.

White columns supporting
the airy roof are slanting,
shaped like a forest,

to represent African justice
traditionally taking place outside
in villages under the trees.

Sculpted opening leaves at the ceiling
are designed to represent
a hopeful future opening out.

The offices of the judges are placed
in the old prison cell blocks.
Torture probably happened in these rooms.

Now, places of terror
have been made into places of justice.
The judges sit, as a strong planned statement,

just where inmates and prisoners did,
reclaiming and transforming
the law and architecture of apartheid.

Outside, there are the 'Great African Steps'
leading up at a gentle incline
to Constitution Square.

Made of the
apartheid prison bricks,
representing brutal injustice,

the Great Steps instead become wider and wider,
symbolising liberation and reconciliation,
leading up and up to the light.

Now is the time to remember Johnny

This poem is a posthumous tribute, personal and public, to a close friend and confidant of 40 years.

Johnny Sachs was a long-time South African anti-apartheid activist; a doctor exiled in London; and a strong supporter of the ANC. A badly damaged heart from rheumatic fever in childhood accompanied him throughout his life (including five open heart surgeries). He returned after the end of apartheid and continued to work for a new progressive South Africa, specialising in developing programmes to deal with HIV/AIDS and promoting social medicine. His well-known brother, Justice Albie Sachs, was imprisoned, exiled and finally car bombed in Mozambique by the previous regime, losing one of his arms and sight in one eye. Justice Sachs later assisted in writing the new Constitution and became one of the first Constitutional Court Judges of the new South Africa, making many internationally celebrated landmark judgments. He retired in 2009. The two brothers, both dedicated in their activism and commitment, came from a left-wing and politically active Jewish family, impassioned in support of workers' rights and African liberation. Johnny died in 2003. This personal tribute is included here with the support, edits and agreement of his brother.

People have gathered
to pay their rich tributes.
They will go on doing so…
His esteemed brother and others
have spoken their pained and beautiful words.
Good friends have come together to hold each other,
in his city.
Johnny was a city person.
Cape Town, London, Cape Town, London,
Cape Town, London,
his two homes, steady between the two,
once exile was over.

Yes, his steadiness.

There was a thing.
His quiet and unassuming wisdom,
never one to make a fuss about himself.
But somehow we all felt
we could not quite live or manage without him.

Now we must…...

*****

I remember you, Johnny, exercising and swimming,
on the Cape Town Clifton Beaches,
laughing, frozen-cold in the Antarctic current.
Or body-boarding at Muizenberg,
decayed and newly multi-racial.
Your memories of the old white days there,
as a nervous young socialist,
resentfully taking photos for a living
of rich Jewish families down from Johannesburg.

*****

I remember waiting for you, Johnny,
outside Parliament in Cape Town,
as you came out, pleased from meetings with Ministers,
trying in your careful way
to make your post-apartheid contribution.

I remember us being greeted by,
and quietly greeting,
Nelson Mandela,
one time with Wolfie.
Mandela slim and svelte then,
already in his 80s.

I remember driving with you, day after day,
around 1960s London
before it was 'the Sixties'.
And we would conspire,
laughing about the conventional people
where we worked and had first met…

I was only 20.
I am not sure that I took your heart operations seriously,
so lightly you spoke of them,
hiding a life-threatening heart condition
and your loneliness in this new grey city of exile.

I could have helped more…..

But we met and laughed and talked
then and always,
over all these 40 years…

*****

Our friendship going on and on,
golden light one time under the Eiffel Tower,
cappuccinos in Regent's Park,
Italian food in Oxford,
too much wine in Franzhoek.

Dear Johnny,
you have been a rock for me
(even from a distance)
as for so many.
I never heard you say a vicious or unkind word
about anyone in all those years.

*****

Your eyes would suddenly light up,
my old dear friend,
at some pleasure.
But you were a solid man,
a man of routine.
Scotch and salted nuts before dinner,
same London apartment....
(I remember it bare and empty,
30 years before it was opulent).

In early retirement, golf and tennis,
bridge and poker.
You measured the cloth of your life.

Before,
there were those long, long hours of work.
Immunology claiming your
scientific life and achievements.

I would rush with you from hospitals
to transport live human kidneys
for transplant operations, through Red Star,

stopping at restaurants afterwards,
you asking the musician to sing
'The Streets of London'.

*****

Always, there were your political colleagues,
your friends and lovers…
Your few very big relationships.
You told me of them all.
As I did in return.

Dear Johnny,
we figured out a unique friendship,
enriching those major life relationships
that engaged us both.

*****

I recall so much so well…
Your studied presentation of political points,
measured way of speaking.

Remembrances of your uneasy childhood,
the 'snakes in the grass' story
that always made me cry.

(Your parents talking together,
anxious about political betrayal
by informants in
the underground struggle
against apartheid.
But you heard it as snakes on your solitary way
across fields to school,
and travelled in cautious frightened hops thereafter.)

Of course, there was always your famous brother,
just eighteen months older,
but without a life-defying illness.
Throughout, you always tried to support him.

Trustworthy in all adversity,
as he was attacked by the government
in South Africa,
in London,
in Maputo.
You travelled there

to bring him back to the UK,
almost dead,
after the car bomb…

*****

And there was your medical wisdom,
helping so many
with assessments and advice.
Never anything sensational…
Much later, there were your travels
in the US, Eastern Europe,
Chile of course, with your last partner.

There was your AIDs work that outlives you,
your TB project
and your joy as the people sang
when the motorbike that you'd funded
bringing their medicine
made it finally through the bush
to their remote African village.

And always the ANC and your wise judgments.

The great and unfinished South African struggle
that defined, dominated
and enclosed your life.

*****

In the beginning and the end of course, your illness.
You were practical and well-informed,
got the best advice about your chances
from doctor friends,
refused to use your health condition to gain kudos,

as I certainly would have,
even if I think I wouldn't...

In recent years it looked as if
the last of many valves clicking away
would see you through.
Many of us became almost complacent,
as we later agreed,
sometimes forgetting that, actually, each day
was a priceless and unlikely gift.

Johnny,
you dealt logically,
no drama,
with massive heart problems,
five open heart surgeries,
political repression, exile,

quietly refusing to be emotional,
to over-state, to promote yourself above others --
to make out that you were in any way unique or special...

But you were.
You were.

Bravery

She had just arrived in Kuala Lumpur,
spread out and sparkling,
with its monster-size twin towers.
Flying in, the air stewards warned not
to bring illegal drugs into the country,
commenting almost in passing
that the mandatory sentence is, well, death.

It is so clean and graceful everywhere.
People are gracious too.
Chinatown has good-smelling food, crowds of tourists.
Then something happens, sudden fear in people's eyes,
several run and hide, as police
burst into the streets, wielding sticks.
People are hit, there is shouting and panic.
She fades out of the way.

She knows it can be hard here,
although it is so gorgeous and captivating.
Her friends are some of the leading activists
on violence against women in the country.
They had sat in her sitting room,
laughed together on Charing Cross Road.
At home here, they are strong-willed and serious.
They risk hostility and attack,
setting up 'domestic violence and health' centres,
taking a brave and tough stand for women.
Feeling a bit anxious, she celebrates them.

Poems of Canada and the death of my mother

Montréal in the Sixties

Dear Canada,
with your lakes and openness,
cool music,
kind-hearted people, welcoming and warm.

It's the second biggest country of them all,
this giant peaceful nation,
a model for the rest of the world

(well, that is if you block out
the ravages of present governments --
right-wing and cost-slashing --
the Alberta tar sands,
the past treatment of Québec,
the First Nations catastrophe...).

But we loved you nonetheless
with your cleanness,
Nova Scotia lakes,
forests to the horizon in Ontario,
the Rockies that dwarf everything else,
trains with six engines,
all pulling together
one behind the other,
to get through the pass.

Most of all, we remember Montréal in the Sixties.
Our wild new politics and music,
psychedelic adventuring,
our clothes transformed with home-sewn elaborations,
our previous attitudes transformed too.
It was a sparkling time,
we scarcely knew what hit us.

But we battled the police to support Québecois rights.
Built community action campaigns
against rapacious developers.
Fought against racism.
Went to gorgeous parties at every turn.

Those of us who were white
from North America or Europe were perhaps
just plain lucky,
thinking of ourselves as revolutionaries,
although we weren't really, I don't suppose.
We ran into new changes and excitement round each corner.

But our group came from all over the world,
the Caribbean, India, Egypt, China, South Africa,
Indonesia, Nicaragua, Peru.
Some friends were later deported
to South Vietnam and Latin American dictatorships
on grounds of left-wing activity.
At least one, I found out, was subsequently assassinated.

When Canada declared the War Measures Act
in Québec in 1970
(believing there was about to be an insurrection),
there were 6,000 soldiers on the streets of Montréal
with bayonets fixed,
tanks on every corner.

Friends came home from work and found the military
trashing their apartment.
Civil liberties and human rights were suspended,
making it clear what precious gifts they are.
Some people I knew hid in cupboards,
their faces blank with terror.

But, other times, life was thrilling.
We would smoke hash.
Go to late-night soul music.
Gather without planning it
at someone's house
for a special breakfast,
Egyptian or Trinidadian perhaps.

We initated co-operatives,
collective daycare centres.
Set up communes with courageous US deserters
and draft resisters in hiding from their country.

I was one of the only whites
at a seminal Black Writers Conference
at which young Black Panthers
with cocked guns and ammunition
surrounded the stage
to protect their exalted ones.
Eldridge Cleaver had dropped underground the week before.

We organised against the Vietnam War.
Contributed to building poor people's movements.
Discovered enthusiastically and all of a sudden
the renewed idea of liberation for women.

We were privileged to be in a position
to transfigure our pasts at every step,

to live in a creative political whirlwind.
We tried to make it all up afresh
throwing out anything conventional,
spontaneity in the air,
late, late nights and music,
shared 3am feasts from Pines delivery
(long closed now),
on Avenue des Pins.

We did make some permanent impacts,
but not that many in the end.

Those of us who stayed in contact still love
that country, that city.
Our city.

Dear Canada,
sitting quietly alongside its mighty neighbour.

Sophisticated Montréal.

Dear days of our far-away youth.

We have lived our lives with exuberance.
But we have always remembered.
They were our best and free days.

They mould us yet.

At Marilyn's House (to my mother)

Arm-in-arm,
we went out that time at Marilyn's house
to see the full moon, swaying sallow-yellow,
in the great and empty Canadian sky.
You needed my help.
We were awed, edging on tearful.

Twenty more full moons you saw.
After ten of those,
Marilyn and I met again for the first time since.
We saw the full moon rise against a Cornish sea.

Ten moons later,
we were together once more.
This time, we walked in the park
beneath a Bristol full moon
as we cared for you, two weeks from death,
a profound symmetry for us all.

Flying back home, Marilyn phoned to say
the moon had not yet waned,
there outside her house,
just as Mum and I remembered,
in the great and empty Canadian sky.

At the last, we held your hands
and cried out to you as you died,
tried and tried to call you back to us.

The desperate lengthening gaps between your rasping
final breaths.
That night was the new moon though.

Now I am back at Marilyn's house

Now I am back at Marilyn's house.
The full moon, adrift in luminous mauve
dries my mouth,
like it does it in these parts.
Crickets fill the air, in the hanging warmth.

That great and empty Canadian sky again,
so clear it hurts.
Edging on tearful,
I stand alone.
Shortly before you died, I started to remind you
of the moon at Marilyn's house
but you didn't need telling.
You knew straight away
breaking in with a weakened, effortful voice
to tell me the story
using the same words I would have,
as I held you in my arms
with death before us.

Edging on tearful
as we remembered together.
But this time, the severing is
of a quite different order.

Now, under the moon at Marilyn's house,
the tears are thick and silent. I stand alone.

Section III
Poems of resolution

The second time at Eleni's

The second time at Eleni's,
the woman swam in moonlight,
they stayed in the delightfully cool olive-store house
with a stone flagged floor,
and the season hadn't quite kicked in yet.
There were visiting dogs and swallows,
the Aegean Sea lapped below the door.
And there were floaty heaps of olive flowers.
They put some in the house.

The man cooked beans (gigantic) and warm potato salad,
pan-roasted stuffed peppers, sheep's cheese and tomatoes,
all with olive oil to slurp up.
They talked about Jack Kerouac.
The sea was aquamarine and purple,
when it wasn't turquoise silver.
The woman remembered another Greek sea
from her youth,
her first shocked sight of the Mediterranean
(but that one was more than 50 years ago).

They were lucky with that big moon,
not so lucky with the siege of kamikaze moths.
But it was warm enough to sit out
by the water at midnight.
They found comforting glow worms
flashing among the olives.
As always, there was the film of stars reflected in the water.

A memoir of India

This is by way of a small thank-you.
It's been a long time coming.
A healing time,

a new beginning.
You can kind of depend on
monumental India to do that, I guess.

II

Well, we have swum
on deserted tropical beaches in the dark,
watched village women make string from coconut.

We have eaten bhel puri at Juhu,
and been given Hindu feast food,
laid out on banana leaves with gold-leaf,

seen moth-eaten elephants
with their bad-tempered mahouts,
and been garlanded in craft collectives.

And we have drunk banana lassi
and been taken unawares
by a sudden offer of chocolate pudding.

In a Katakhali place, we listened to tabla and sitar
by crashing waves,
and paddled in the monsoon.

We have travelled on city trains at rush times,
not for the faint-hearted,

and hung on in auto-rickshaws.

We have cowered on speeding country buses,
overtaking in impossible places,
as people and bikes and dogs scatter from their path.

III

And it goes on and on, the list.
In Fort Kochi (which everyone still calls Cochin),
we watched the Chinese fishing nets working,

drank fresh watermelon juice at midnight,
and secret beer from teapots
("would you like some special tea, madam?").

We negotiated with clever Kashmiri salesmen,
each one assuring us that his was the only
honest, decent shop in town, not like all the others.

We were taken by boat on faintly smelling lakes,
with tiny silver fish jumping,
to have Ayurvedic massages.

In Bombay, we drank chai
at dark market cafes in backstreets
where boys who were not in school,

and maybe never had been,
carried 10 glasses of local water,
with a finger down inside each glass.

We bought gilded alphonso mangoes
and pawpaws 18 inches long,
and watched cricket on the Oval Maidan,

by the Colonial High Court building
on to which, long ago,
a local stone mason carved in secret

a one-eyed monkey
to make fun of British justice,
without the British noticing.

IV

In Kerala,
where previous communist governments
have left their mark,

schools, colleges and hospitals everywhere,
we have been kept awake late by firecrackers
at a glittering festival,

seen giant crabs racing in the dark,
and chameleons, two feet long by our cabin,
pretending not to be there.

We have watched prawn fishermen
in wood canoes,
wearing just their mundu and head-rag,

casting their circular nets,
and then walking in the water beside their boats,
as they always have.

And we have covered ourselves in Deet
and been bitten anyway,
seen the dawn over bath-warm backwaters.

In Maharashtra, we watched a mendicant
beating his bare body with deafening cracks
of a golden jeweled whip (a trick for sure),

marched with an enormous demonstration
of Dalit and tribal people,
who had travelled for four days just to get there.

We visited an activist village
where impoverished residents
have held a Petro-Chemical company at bay for years,

and routinely greet other people with a
raised clenched fist and a laugh,
instead of a Namaste.

V

India for us
was full of the most generous-spirited people,
women in dazzling colours,

bright pinks, yellows, turquoise,
young men with moustaches,
asking us to pose with them for photos.

And so, 'our' India,
a privilege to be there.
For us, it's been a long time coming.

Paris, London, Bristol, home

If you have children, you are seared forever,
in your every breath, every thought, in the soul of you,
the massive love you can't explain to the child-free.
My long-adult children, gracious and talented,
weaving their individual paths to light up the world
in Paris, London, Bristol,
cities resplendent in culture,
catastrophic pasts of colonialism and slavery,
new multi-racial populations.
The empires have come home.

I have too.
To love and connection,
deep and nurturing,
to those fine small moments,
new futures, new children,
new and old friends
and people to pass on to,
to not be forgotten,
to leave behind memories,

cirrus clouds of humanness
and our lives well lived.

Also by the author

Books of poetry
Rive Gauche: Women poets in Bristol (edited with Pat VT West and Shelley Allen). 1998. Bristol: Rive Gauche Publishers.

What she also did was (edited with Pat VT West) 2009. Bristol: Rive Gauche Publishers.

Individual poems in a variety of publications.

Professional Publications
Overall: approximately 125 publications by Professor Gill Hague on violence against women. These include books, practice guides, international and national reports, professional papers, scholarly papers, book chapters, and activist and government guidance.

Books:
Domestic Violence: Action for Change (with Ellen Malos). Third edition. 2005. Cheltenham: New Clarion Press.
First edition. 1993. Second edition. 1998.
New opportunities, old challenges: The Multi-agency Approach to Domestic Violence (with Nicola Harwin and Ellen Malos). 2000. London: Whiting and Birch.
Children's Perspectives on Domestic Violence (with Audrey Mullender, Liz Kelly, Ellen Malos, Linda Regan and Umme Imam). 2002. London: Sage.
Don't hurt my Mum (with Audrey Mullender et al). 2003. London: Young Voice.
Is Anyone Listening? (with Audrey Mullender and Rosemary Aris). 2003. London: Routledge.
Empowering Women in Communities to deal with Domestic Violence: A Manual for Community Organisers, Mumbai, India (with Lynn Sardinha, Ellen Malos, Helen Joseph and Mary Alphonse). 2006.
Understanding Children Exposed to Domestic Violence: A Manual for School Educators, Mumbai, India (with ditto). 2006. Both manuals: Mumbai, India: Nirmala Niketan / British Council.

Disabled women and Domestic Violence: Making the links (with Ravi Thiara). 2009. London: Jessica Kingsley Press.
Still Hurting, Still Forgotten: Adult experiences of domestic violence from childhood. (with Ann Harvey and Kathy Willis). 2011. London: Jessica Kingsley Press.
Honour-based Violence in Iraqi Kurdistan and the UK (with Nazand Begikhani and Aisha Gill). 2015. Devon: Ashgate.

Selected other major publications and guide books:
The Silent Pain: Domestic Violence 1945-1970 (with Claudia Bernard). 1996. Bristol: The Policy Press.
Children and Refuges (with Liz Kelly, Ellen Malos, Thangam Debonnaire and Audrey Mullender). 1996. Bristol: WAFE.
Multi-agency Work and Domestic Violence (with Ellen Malos and Wendy Dear). 1996. Bristol: The Policy Press
Tackling Domestic Violence: A guide to developing multi-agency initiatives (with Ellen Malos). 1996. Bristol: The Policy Press
Canadian Innovations and Violence against Women (with Liz Kelly and Audrey Mullender). 2000. Bristol: The Policy Press.
Home Office Briefings: a) *The voices of survivors* and b) *Multi-agency initiatives* (with Audrey Mullender). 2000. London: Home Office.
From Good Intentions to Good Practice: Good Practice Guidelines (with Cathy Humphreys, Marianne Hester, and Audrey Mullender, Hilary Abrahams and Pam Lowe). York: JRF.
Professionals by Experience: Practice Guide (with Audrey Mullender). 2003. Bristol: Women's Aid.
Immigration, Marriage and Domestic Violence (with Geetanjali Gangoli, Helen Joseph, Mary Alphonse) 2007. Mumbai: British Academy.
Marriage and Bride-price in Uganda (with Ravi Thiara). 2009. Uganda: Mifumi.
Making the Links: Disabled Women and Domestic Violence.
a) *Report* and b) *Good Practice Guidance* (with Ravi Thiara, Pauline Magowan and Audrey Mullender). 2008. Bristol: Women's Aid.
Honour-based Violence and Honour-based Killings in Iraqi Kurdistan and in the Kurdish Diaspora in the UK (in English and in Kurdish) (with Nazand Begikhani, Aisha Gill and Kawther Ibraheem. 2010. Erbil, Kurdistan: Kurdistan Regional Government.

Index of First Lines (and Poem Titles)